*Reprint from the "École Française d'Extrême-Orient."*

# NOTES

ON THE

# ANCIENT GEOGRAPHY OF BURMA

## (I)

BY

C. DUROISELLE, M.R.A.S.

LECTURER IN PĀLI, RANGOON COLLEGE

RANGOON

OFFICE OF THE SUPERINTENDENT, GOVERNMENT PRINTING, BURMA

1906

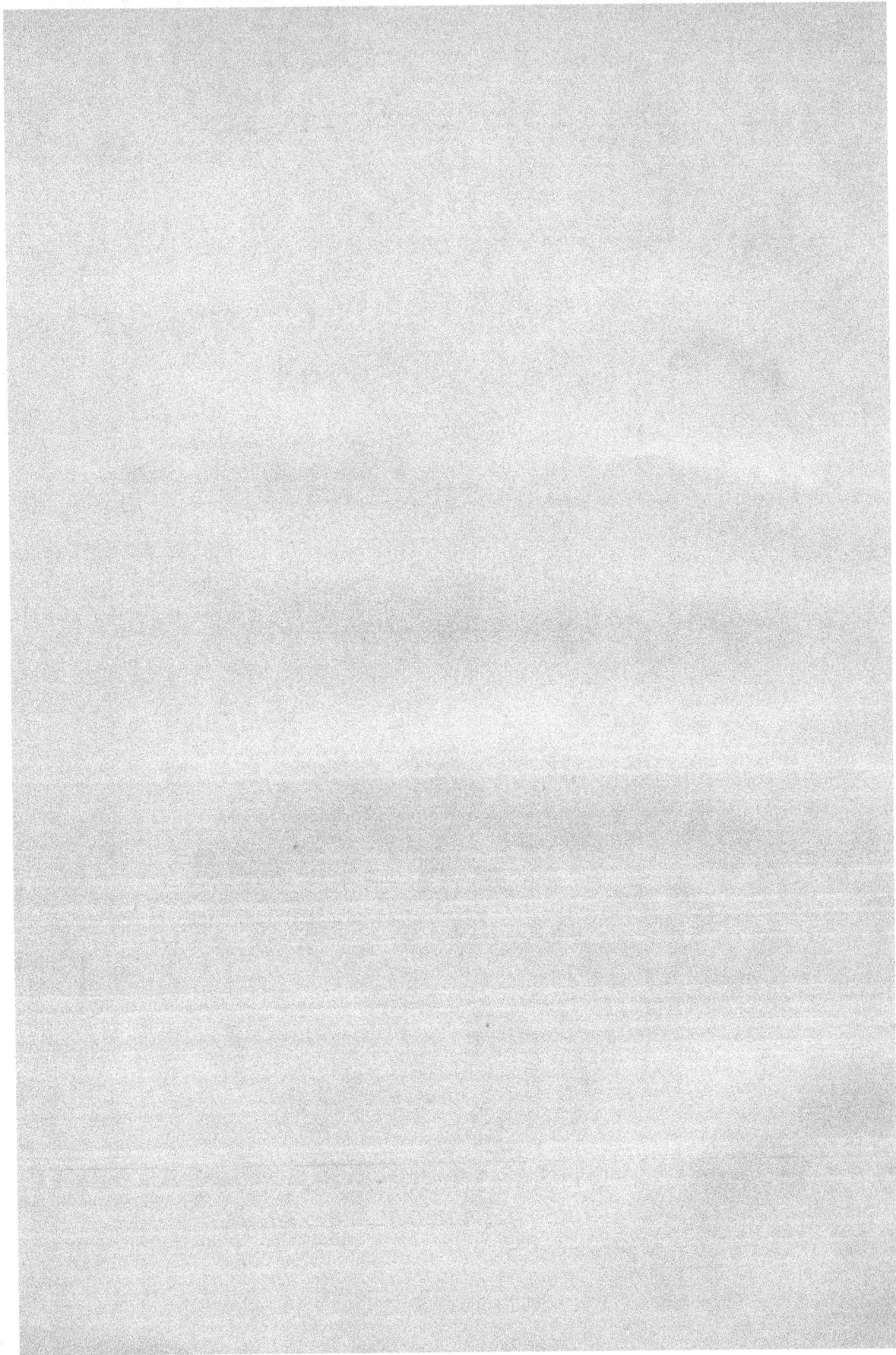

# NOTES ON THE ANCIENT GEOGRAPHY OF BURMA.

THE *Punnovāda-sutta* of the *Samyutta-nikāya* is found, almost word for word, in the Sanskrit version of the celebrated Legend of Pur*n*a, as translated by Burnouf from the Divyāvadāna.[1] The Pâli Sutta does not give us any further information concerning this interlocutor of the Buddha; but the commentaries or *Atthakathā* give, as a rule, the history of the persons mentioned in the texts.[2] Consequently, while looking over the voluminous commentary on the Saññyutta, I have found therein the Legend of Pu*nn*a (Sanskrit Pūr*n*a) such as it is known to the Southern School of Buddhism, or, at least, that part of the legend which the commentators have thought fit to insert in their work: for if the *sutta* itself seems to be but an extract (unless one prefers to see in it the nucleus round which the legend later on developed itself), the commentary gives to the careful reader the impression that it (the commentary) is but an abridgment from which are omitted secondary incidents known to the Sanskrit version. Two points seem to me to admit of no doubt: on the one hand, the story existed before the evolution peculiar to Northern Buddhism, since the *Purnāvadāna* contains the Pâli *sutta;* on the other, it had remained quite popular amongst the Southern Buddhists up to the time of the redaction of the Saññyutta*tth*akathā, for this commentary introduces the two brothers in the story with the words "*ete dve Bhātaro,*" without these "two brothers" having yet been mentioned. This detail confirms me in the opinion that the compilers whose intention was merely to recall that part of the story relating to the country of Sunāparanta, have not judged necessary to reproduce in its

(¹) *Samyutta or Saññyutta-nikāyā*, ed. Feer, Vol. IV, page 60; *Divyāvadāna*, ed. Cowell and Neil, pages 24—55. Burnouf, *Introduction*, ed. 1844, pages 235—276; ed. 1876, page 209—245.

(²) Most of these commentaries have not yet been edited and are therefore unknown to scholars in Europe.

entirety a legend already well known and such probably, except a few unimportant details, as we have it in the *Divāyvadāna*. The fact is that the Divyāvadāna is unknown in Burma, [1] but in the "*History of the Foot-Print*," [2] we find another legend forming a kind of introduction to that of the *Sannyutta* commentary, and from this we may infer that the Sanskrit version has not been altogether unknown in Burma. The Legend of Pu*nn*a contains,

(¹) We have reasons to believe that Sanskrit was known in Burma before Pâli. The Burmese of the 10th and 11th centuries dispels all doubts on this point: for in the inscriptions of that period are found words clearly derived from Sanskrit, and not only technical terms, but words which must have already been in popular use, such as, for example, *prassad*, from Sanskrit *prāsāda*, the Pâli being *pāsāda*; *Sakrā* = Sanskrit *Cakra* (Pâli *sakka*). After its introduction into Pagan, Pâli was studied with great fervour, and the first outcome of these studies, about one century after the fall of Thatôn, was the *Sadda-niti*, a grammar of the *Tripitaka*, and the most comprehensive in existence. Forchhammer gives 1156 A.D. as the date of this work; but Aggava*m*sa, the author, himself says that it was completed in 1154 A.D. Now, Aggava*m*sa, in the second part of his grammar, the *Dhātumālā* or "Garland of Roots," gives here and there the equivalent Sanskrit forms. It is therefore plausible to suppose that Sanskrit existed at Pagan in the 11th century at least and was scientifically studied before Pâli, for the first work in the latter language written in Burma bases itself on Sanskrit grammar to explain a few Pâli forms. Another proof is the use, in the dates of the 11th and the 12th centuries of the Hindu astronomical terminology; for instance, Asan=Acvini (1054 A.D.); Mrikkasō=Mrgaciras (1081 A.D.), etc. The *Siddhanta*, then, must have been known in Pagan anterior to those dates. Moreover, certain names of places and rivers indicate a familiarity, very probably already secular in Anorata's time with Hindu mythology; to give but one example: on the banks of the Irrawaddy (=Pâli, *Erāvati*= Sanskrit *airāvati*), the legend of the famous elephant *airāvata* is well known. Other proofs are less sure: thus Mr. Taw Sein Ko (*Notes on the Kalyāni Inscriptions*) speaks of bricks found at Tagoung and at Pagan itself, inscribed with legends in Sanskrit and older than the introduction of Southern Buddhism in Pagan; but Phayre says (*History of Burma*, page 14) that the legends were in Pâli. As it is very difficult to procure any of these bricks, I cannot settle this question; it is to be doubted whether even the Archæological Museum in Rangoon possesses any; at least, none of these short legends has ever yet been deciphered. No Sanskrit inscription has yet been found in Burma: Dr. Führer, it is true, says (*Notes on an Archæological tour in Upper Burma*) that he discovered two at Tagoung: but nothing more was ever heard of these two lithic inscriptions, of such a paramount importance if they do really exist, which I doubt very much.

(²) In Burmese: ရွှေစက်တော်သမိုင်း (*Rhve-cak-to-Samôn*). The principal temples and pagodas each have their *samôn* or "history." These histories, amid the overgrowth of marvellous tales, contain very precious historical informations, and give dates, which are generally exact, of contemporary events. Some of these *samôn* have been utilized for the compilation of the Mahārājavan; but most of them are crumbling to pieces in the dust of monasteries.

according to the Burmese, the history of the two imprints of the Buddha's left foot, which he, the Master—after having, as it is written, spent one week in the magnificent monastery built with red sandal wood—left, one, on the bank of the မန်းချောင်း (Man : Khyo*n*)[1] stream, the other on the summit of the သစ္စဗန် (Saccaban) Hill,[2] whose foot is washed by the said stream. This hill, consecrated by the Buddha's presence, is situated near Saku, in the Minbu District, which is itself comprised in the Province of Aparanta or Sunāparanta ; for the Burmese have appropriated to themselves this name at the expense of the Konkan and apply it to the region which stretches, on the right bank of the Irrawaddy, behind and above Pagan. They have not the least doubt that Sunāparanta (Sanskrit Çronāparānta) of the Saññutta*tth*akathā, is the very same as the Burmese Province called by that name. The Legend is quoted in the *Mahārājavan* when recording the foundation of Prome ;[3] therein we are told that Vā*n*ijagāma is none else but the village called လယ်ကိုင်း (Lê Kine) by the Burmese and that it is situated in the Province of Sunāparanta.

(1) "Charmed-stream" ; *Man* = *manta* (Sanskrit *mantra*) : it is the Nammadā of the legend.

(2) Pron. *Thissaban* = *Saccabandha* : further on, we shall see the origin of this name.

(3) *Mahārājavan*, Vol. I, pages 167—168. Prome is written ပြည် Prañ, by the Burmese and the Arakanese. The Burmese pronounce Pyī and Pyè, the Arakanese, Fri. But the Môn (Talaings) write this word and pronounce it ပြောင် Prôn, and ပြန် Prawn. It is then in Talaing documents that we must look for the origin of this name, the signification of which I do not know ; * the Talaings I have consulted could not give me any information on this point. Some, however, told me that this word ought to be written, "Prôm" (pronounced exactly as Prome) ; this word means "crushed, destroyed," and Criksetra has, they say, been so called since its destruction by the Môn (Talaings) some years before the foundation of Pagan. But this etymology is not worth stopping to consider. Namantā, in the Rājava*n*, is given as the name of the stream, which is also sometimes called after the Nāga's name ; but Namantā is but a corruption of Nammadā.

* It has been urged that "*Prome*" is derived from "Brahma" ; this may very well be. But it is remarkable that none of the nations that have known this old city call it by a name derived, according to their phonetics, from "Brahma." It was better known to them as *Criksetra*, or its modified equivalents Phonetically, the Burmese and Arakanese ပြည် Prañ, cannot stand for "Brahma," and their pronunciation of it differs still more widely.

Now, the *Paganrājavan*[1] tells us that Lê Kine or Vā*n*ijagāma is in the Province of Pūrantappa. This name, Pūrantappa, applies to the region already mentioned in manuscripts, and is unknown to the majority of the Burmese, even to those well educated. However the case may be, the Legend, as it is understood by them, is interesting, in that it is a very clear example of the origin of the artificial geography of Burma, in the fabrication of which some texts have been flagrantly distorted and their sense deliberately misunderstood. Before going into this question of fabrication, let me be allowed to give here the Burmese legend which forms a kind of introduction to that of Pu*nn*a.

In olden times, there was, in the Island of ဟိုင်းကြီးကျွန်း[2] (Hô*n*-kri: kyvan), a cultivator who possessed a magnificent bull; this bull, as strong as he was beautiful, was savage and vicious; no one but his master dared approach him: to do so would have been to run to a certain death. He had become the terror of the village, for he pursued and tore into pieces everything he found in his way, beasts and men. He had already carried mourning and sorrow into many families, and the fear of him had come to such a pitch that all work in the fields was at last neglected. This state of things could not last much longer, for famine and ruin were spreading their ravages in the neighbouring villages as well. The villagers assembled and, after a short discussion, unanimously resolved to destroy the ferocious animal. They apprized the owner of their intention, leaving him the choice to go somewhere else and take his bull with

Moreover, the word Brahma is well known to the Burmese, and is of very frequent occurrence in their sacred literature; it is always and rightly written: ဗြဟ္မ (brahma); according to Burmese phonetics ဗြဟ္မ might become ဗြန်း, (bram), but never, by any rule, ပြည်. It is strange that, possessing already the name in its proper form (ဗြဟ္မ, brahma), they should have altered it to ပြည် (prañ) for the city's name and to မြန်မာ (Mranmā) for their own national appellation.

The Talaing for "Brahma" is ဗြုမ် (Brom, *pron.* Prām), a word extensively used in their literature, for they were under brahmanical influence for centuries; but they too, rejecting the proper, ready-made and well-known appellation (ဗြုမ်), call *Criksetra* by a name (ပြန်) which, according to Talaing phonetics, cannot be a derivation of "Brahma."

(1) Page 37 of the manuscript in my possession (page 3 of the 2nd chap.).

(2) One of the names by which Cape Negrais is known to the Burmese.

him. The farmer, who was attached to his fields, allowed them, after some demur, to do as they pleased. The villagers then armed themselves with sticks, pitchforks, bows, etc., and, after a quasi-homeric fight, brought the bull to his death ; they cut up the carcase there and then, and distributed its flesh. The happy event of the bull's death was, on the evening of the very same day, celebrated by a great feast, of which the enormous animal's flesh formed one of the most delicate dishes. Unfortunately, every violent act, however justifiable, has its retribution ; in consequence, all those who had taken part in the feast were born again in the forests of Sunāparanta, in Upper Burma. Some became bisons, some deer, rabbits, antelopes, wild-boars, etc., and the bull, their victim, became a hunter whose humble dwelling was a hut on the slope of the Maku*l*a Hill (the same which received, later on, the name of Saccabandha). This hill is now known also as "the Hunter's Hill."[1] His arrows never erred ; he roamed in the woods and on

(1) မုဆိုးတောင် (Mu-cho-to*n*), near Lê-kô*n* ( ထယ်ကိုင်း), in the Minbu District. The legend has been perpetuated in the names of certain hills ; for instance, the hill where he dried his skins is the "stretched-out-hides Hill," သားရေကြက်တောင် Sā-re-krak-to*n* ; the one where he strung his bow is to-day : လင်တင် ကုန်း Lim ( = le= လေး) -ta*n*-kun ; the forest wherein he pursued the hare is known as : ယုန်ကြည့်တော ,Yun-krañ-to ; and so forth, *cf.* the legend given by Sir George Scott (*Upper Burma Gazetteer*, II, iii page 163). I do not know where Sir George has taken this story from ; he has, I suppose, translated it from the Sa*m*ô*n*, for it is essentially the same ; but, surely, the dates mentioned are impossible. The Burmese always give the correct dates, as they are entered in the Mahārājava*n*, a work found everywhere in Burma ; they perhaps might make an error of some years, but never one of several centuries, as Sir George does, and the dates which he gives are not those of the Sa*m*ô*n*. He says that "in 248 B.E. (*Burmese Era*, that is to say, C*aka*, = 886 A.D.) Alaung Sithu, king of Pagan, visited the Shwe-zet-taw," but Alaung Sithu became king only in 1085 A.D., according to Phayre. In Vol. II, part ii, 307, he writes : "The legend . . . . says that king Alaung Sithu, in 470 B.E. = 1108 A.D., left Minbu and went to Saku, then called Ramawadi ;" the difference between the two dates given for one and the same reign is consequently 222 years ! The date 1108 is not that given by the Sa*m*ô*n* for the visit of this king to Minbu, but C*aka* 454 = 1092 A.D. On the page already quoted, a few lines lower down (Vol. II, iii page 163), he says : "In 427 B.E. = 1065 A.D. the king Patama (Pa*th*ama) Min Gaung made a dedication of lands to the Shwe-zet-taw." But Pa*th*ama Min Gaung ascended the throne only in 1401 A.D., and the Sa*m*ô*n* tells us that, in C*aka* 763 (= 1401 A.D.), this king visited the famous foot-prints ; here, the difference is 336 years !

the hills, playing great havoc among their wild inhabitants, whose flesh he sold to his customers.

It happened the One-thousand-eyed Çakra, looking down on the earth, descried the hunter of Sunāparanta, whose bow had caused the useless death of so many innocent creatures, and his heart was moved with pity. He also perceived in the heart of the cruel hunter, as a fire mouldering under the ashes, a disposition towards spirituality which would make of him a great saint if he could be induced to embrace religious life. He, then, assumed the appearance of a hunter, descended to Sunāparanta and hid himself near a spot by which the destroyer had to pass. This hill is well known as Sakrāpun-ton (သကြားပုန်းတောင်). The Sunāparanta hunter appeared; Çakra greeted him: "Friend, whither are you going?" "A hunting," replied the other, "for I must provide venison for my customers." Çakra, with his divine eloquence, shewed him the cruelty of thus killing innocent victims, and the terrible torments which such a profession had in store for him in the course of his future existences. "What!" exclaimed the astonished hunter, "are not you yourself a hunter? Do you not, too, make a living, in pursuing the deer in the forests?" What a fine sermon you are preaching me!" "My friend," answered Çakra,

One would be inclined to think that Sir George Scott follows a local legend giving false dates; but such is not the case, for the legend of the *Upper Burma Gazetteer* is merely that of the Samôn abridged, and as the dates of the Samôn agree with those of the Chronicles, one cannot understand these glaring errors in so serious a work. However, on the following page (II, iii page 164), under the heading Shwe-zi-gôn, he gives a date better in accordance with facts. There he writes: "It is said that the founder of the Shwezi-gôn is Prince Saw-Lu, a son of Anawyata Min Zau (Anuruddha-man-co), who visited Pindalè (now Minthalè) in 421 B.E. (= 1059 A.D.). Phayre makes Saw-Lu die in in 1057 A.D. after a reign of five years, which is, according to the inscriptions, altogether wrong. Most of the dates given by Phayre (*History of Burma*) for the eleventh and twelfth centuries are inexact, and this part of his History must be read with great caution. As a matter of fact, the Chronicles themselves do not agree on those dates. For the beginning of Anorata's reign, the Mahārājavan gives 1017 A.D., and this is the date generally accepted; the old edition of the same work gives 967; the Svè Cun Kyo Tan (ရွှေစဉ်ကျောက်တင်), 1002 A.D. the Pagan Rājavan gives 999. Now, there is an inscription dated 984 A.D. erected by Anorata and speaking of a relic brought back from Thaton. All the other dates are viciated by this one. The date of his death, 1059, is confirmed by the inscriptions. The date of the fall of Thaton will perhaps have also to be corrected, although the Kalyāni gives 1057. The Talaing Chronicle

"my case is very different from yours. You kill all the animals you meet with, even when you are no longer in need of meat. I, on the contrary, with this infallible bow, scour the Himalayas in search of flying-deer, whose skin, sold to kings, brings me an immense profit. I kill not for the sole pleasure of killing. I came into these parts in pursuit of a certain flying-deer. Help me to find it. Here, take this my unerring bow and give me yours, and, if you find the deer, shoot it down." The hunter took Çakra's bow, and the latter disappeared among the trees. The divine weapon looked like a toy; but, what was not his astonishment, when, despite all his efforts and his almost superhuman strength, he did not succeed in bending it! In vain did he groan, and sweat and swear: the bow remained as rigid as the trunk of a tree centuries old. The time went swiftly by and no animal was killed, and his customers were waiting for venison. Tired, dispirited, he sat down. Çakra, still disguised as a hunter, appeared again to him. "My bow is not easy to bend, is it? Well! You will be able to bend it as easily as your own on one condition. You must promise to kill only deer one day, and the day after only does. On this trifling condition, you may keep my bow, which is matchless; for it belongs to me, Çakra!" The hunter agreed, hastily took the bow and went about looking for deer; but on that day, he

and incriptions, which I hope to be in a position to decipher before long, *will doubtless throw a flood of light on these so important questions, as well as on the question, no less interesting, of the relations of Cambodia with the countries of the Irrawaddy Delta, relations absolutely ignored in Burmese Annals.

* The Talaing or Môn language has not yet been studied scientifically in the light of comparative philology; there are gaps in the history of Burma and Pegu (Rāmañña) that will be filled probably only when the Talaing chronicles have been read and translated; so, the affinities between the Môn and Khmer are still to be philologically established—the author, in the course of his studies of the Môn and Cambodian languages has been struck by the strong internal evidence of their relationship; the name "Môn-Annam" for this family of languages will have to be abandoned, as the Annamese has, from internal evidence, nothing in common with the Talaing and the Khmer.

The writer has now a Talaing Grammar and Chrestomaty nearly completed. The enlightened help of Government, would, in this matter, greatly facilitate the prosecution of his studies and the early publication of their results.

found only does; on the morrow be looked for does, but perceived deer only. He then understood Çakra's stratagem and, bound by a solemn promise which be dared not break, he gave up hunting, became a hermit and retired to a hill. From that day, he was known under the name of Thissa ban (=*sacca*, promise, and *bandha*, bound), and consequently the hill on which he lived received the same name. But he did not know the true religion (*viz.*, Buddhism), and he preached in Sunāparanta a false doctrine,[1] thus causing the people to be in danger of falling into hell. Near that spot, in the village called Vā*n*ija, lived two brothers, merchants, Mahāpu*n* and Cū*l*apu*n* . . . . . . Here the Samô*n* gives, more or less faithfully, the story in the Saññyutta*tth*akathā.[2]

If, now, we compare this legend and the translation of the Pāli text (*cf. infra* p 15), which is its sequel, with the story of the *Divyāvadāna*, many points of resemblance and divergence become apparent. All the long story of the two brothers up to the departure of the elder one to Sāvatthi is unknown to the Samôn and is not given by the commentators on the *Punnovāda-sutta*. The only point of resemblance between the legend of the *Samôn* and that of the Divyāvadāna is the hunter who becomes a hermit and subsequently a saint (*arhat*); and still, neither the manner nor the instrument of his conversion is the same. But this slight resemblance is enough to make one think that, at a certain time, the Sanskrit version was not unknown in Burma. As is almost always the case, the Pāli is more sobre of miraculous happenings than the Sanskrit, and these happenings are precisely the very points whereon the two versions differ. For instance, when, on the invitation of Pu*nn*a, Gotama goes to Vā*n*ijagāma, the 499 monks accompanying him are carried through the sky in kiosques; the *Divyāvadāna* makes them go there by means of wings, or riding on fantastic animals, and even in pots and vases. The Saññyutta*tth*a-kathā speaks of only one *nāga*, but the Sanskrit, of five-hundred, every one of whom creates a river unto himself in order to go to

(1) Are we to see in this "false doctrine" a remembrance of that *religion*, a medley of Mahāyānism, tantraism and Nāga-worship which prevailed in the Irrawaddy Valley before the introduction of Hīnayānist Buddhism into Pagan and the priests of which were the Ari? This *religion* disappeared only in the fifteenth century, and has left very deep traces, not yet obliterated, in the beliefs and customs of the Burmese.

(2) *Vide infra*, p. 15, the text and its translation.

Sūrpāraka, etc. Notwithstanding these differences, the story is, on the whole, the same, and probably originated from the same source. The Sinhalese also have this legend, but they seem to know both versions; for in the fragments translated by Hardy,[1] Sūrpāraka, unknown to the Pāli text, is mentioned, and so is the river Narmadā (Nammadā), of which the *Divyāvadāna* does not speak. In fine, the two imprints of the Buddha's foot, which appear to form the one important point in the legend, are unknown to the compilers of the Sanskrit work.

My intention is not to write a treatise on the ancient geography of Burma, but merely to point out the arbitrary way in which some Indian place-names have been transplanted in Burma, in spite even of explicit texts The Legend of Punna furnishes a very clear example of this manner of fabricating ancient kingdoms and of giving to relatively modern towns an air of hoary antiquity.

Mr. Burgess[2] asks himself how it is that most towns and even mere villages in Burma have two names, [3] one indigenous,

(1) Spence Hardy, *Manual of Buddhism*, ed., 1853, pages 57, 209 and 259-260.

(2) *Indian Antiquary*, Vol. XXX, pages 387-388.

(3) Some towns have many more than two names. In the *Paganrājavan* thirteen names of Pagan are enumerated: Pokkārāma, Arimaddanā, Punnāgāma, Tampavati, Sīripaccayā, Sampunnāgāma, Pandupalāsa, Nagaruttama, Paramapura, Tampadesa, Velurākama (Velukārāma?), Samādhinagara, Pokkan (pron. Paukkan, from which the Burmese made Pukan = Pagan). The *Paganrājavan* gives the following etymologies, which teach us nothing concerning the etymology of "Pugam": "The Buddha having in relation to a *pok* tree (pron. *pauk, butea*), foretold the foundation of Pagan, the town was called "the *pok* garden" (*Pokkārāma*). It was named Arimaddanā because its kings always crushed their enemies. In Pagan, Brahmins (*punna*) lived in considerable numbers; they were traders and treasurers to the king, hence its name of Punnāgāma. (Another tradition says that the city was so called on account of its possessing large quantities of gold, silver and precious things; *punna* = full of. This derivation cannot stand; the first is probably the true one, for the Burmese have always known the Brahmins under the name of *punna*; Punnāgāma is one of the oldest and best known names of Pagan, and it shows, in an incontestable manner, the Indian influence in the 'city of Mien.') It was called Tampavati, Tampadesa and Pandupalāsa on account of the reddish colour of its soil; Sīripaccayā, because of its glory and magnificence; Sampunnāgāma, because its inhabitants were devoted (lit., full of, sampannā) to the three Jewels: the Buddha, the Doctrine and the Church; Nagaruttama, 'The Famous,' on account of its faith and piety. It was

the other Pāli or Sanskrit. I think this fictitious geography has had its origin in the national vanity, and above all, in adulation of courtiers, both Burmese and Indian, and also of historians, who could imagine nothing more likely to minister to the religious bigotry of kings, than to make them rule over provinces recalling, at every step, the Buddha's Life and the early history of Buddhism. This fabrication may also have originated in the intense religious fervour of the two or three centuries which followed the introduction of the Hinayāna into Pagan. In fact, what more natural, at a time of the religious effervescence of a new faith, than to re-name according to the holy books, and as occasions presented themselves, cities and villages and in so doing to transfer to them the numerous legends of the *Atthakathās*, sanctifying, so to say, the whole country, with the supposed presence of the Master? I think it is useless to search for more profound reasons regarding the origin of this apocryphal geography. Royal boastfulness and religious bigotry must have been, I believe, the two most powerful factors in this geographical deception.

As I have already said, the Legend of Pu*nn*a, among a thousand others, furnishes us with a convincing proof of this: for the Pāli text makes it very clear that neither the Sunāparanta, nor the Nammadā, nor the Vā*n*ijagāma of the legend, are the places and the stream known under these names in Burma. The Si*n*halese

called Paramapura, 'the Excellent City,' because of its numerous white elephants On account of its powerful kings it was named Samādhinagara. The name Ve*l*urākama (Ve*l*ukārāma) it received from the extensive bamboo jungles which surrounded it. Pokkan is but an abbreviation of Pokkārāma."

The name "Pugāma" in the Kalyā*n*i Inscriptions is not mentioned in the *Paganrājavan*: According to the rules of Burmese phonetics, Pugāma would necessarily become Pugan, long *ā* being never pronounced and rarely noted before a final consonant. I know not what Pugāma signifies; but I am inclined to believe that King Dhammaceti pālicized the word Pugan (Pagan). Lokānanda is also given as one of the names of Pagan, and this brings the number of its names to fourteen.

Tagoung is called: Sa*n*ghassara*tth*a, Sa*m*sayapura, Pancāla. Prome: Crik *s*etra, Vanavāsi, Pa*tth*anāpati, Varapati, Pu*nn*avati. Arakan is known as: Rāmmāvati, Rakkhapura, Meghavati, Dhaññavati and Dvāravati (this last name is also applied to the Southern Shan States and to Siam). Manipur is: Nāgasyanta and Nāgapura. Kale becomes Rājagaha. Rangoon is known as Ukkalāpa and Verikkhaya.

having a Foot-Print, it was not proper that the Burmese should have none. An imaginary mark on any rock, having more or less the form of a foot, was a sufficient reason for transplanting bodily the scene of the story of Pu*nn*a in a wild spot, and for making this spot a holy place of pilgrimage.

I do not know the exact time at which the name of Sunāparanta was given to the country extending behind Pagan, on the right bank of the Irrawaddy; but it cannot be earlier than the thirteenth century, or perhaps the end of the twelfth. The inscriptions of the eleventh and those of the twelfth century do not mention it. It is very remarkable that the inscriptions of these two centuries and even many belonging to the thirteenth, are composed in very sober language and are singularly free from those lists of kingdoms and empires, in which the kings of the subsequent centuries, in particular those of Ava and Amarapura, so much delighted. From the fact that I could not find this name of Sunāparanta in the most ancient inscriptions, [1] I would not absolutely affirm that it did not exist at that period (eleventh—twelfth centuries), but its absence at least inclines one to think so. This name, then, does not seem to be so ancient in Burma as has been believed up to now.[2] As to the form *Sonāparanta*: "This quasi-classical name of Indian origin, used in the Burmese Court in State documents and formal enumerations of the style of the king," [3] is absolutely unknown to the Burmese. They always write it Sunāparanta,

(1) The most ancient inscription found up to the present was engraved by Anorata-ma*n*-co, and is dated *Caka* 346 = (984 A.D.). It was engraved on the occasion of the building of a shrine for a hair of Buddha, brought back from Thaton. Earnest researches will perhaps bring to light some others more ancient still.

(2) The *Paganrājavan* expressly says (page 37): "The spot whereon Cū*l*apu*n* built the monastery of red sandalwood in Pūrantappa is now known as: Lê-kô*n* (လယ်ကိုင်း)." Thus, Pūrantappa comprised: Lê-kô*n*, Saku (စကု), So*n*-svap (သောင်ဆွပ်), which are subsequently located in Sunāparanta. Purantappa and Sunāparanta designate, therefore, the same province: the first of these names is very nearly unknown now, and seems to be the most ancient. The *Samôn* (သမိုင်း), not perceiving that these two names applied to the same region, gives them (page 23) as the names of two distinct provinces; it is a nonsensical blunder.

(3) Yule's *Hobson-Jobson*, ed. 1903, page 852, col. I.

and give it a very different etymology, as we shall presently see.

The Pāli text of the legend has certainly not in view the Sunāparanta of Burma, but the Konkan, the Western country: Aparanta, as, in fact, the Burmese themselves also call Sunāparanta; the Divyāvadāna calls the Konkan "Çronāparānta." [1] In Sunāparanta flows the Mammadā river (Sanskrit, Narmadā) which is none else but the modern Nerbudda, which throws its waters in the Gulf of Khambat.[2] The Sūrpāraka of *Divyāvadāna* is surely no other place but the Vāṇijagāma of the Pāli version. Vāṇijagāma would perhaps be better translated by "the town, or village, of the merchants." Now, Sūrpāraka, the Suppārakapaṭṭana mentioned in the *Mahāvamsa*, was a great trading port and the entrepôt of Western India; [3] it was then, *par excellence*, a *vāṇijagāma*, a merchant's city or mercantile town.

According also to the Pāli legend, Vāṇijagāma was a sea-port, since Cuḷapuṇṇa embarks there to "cross the sea." Sūrpāraka is situated at the estuary of the Nerbudda, and there also, the commentators on the Puṇṇovādā-sutta locate Vāṇijagāma; these two names, therefore, designate but one and the same town, situated near the mouth of a river in the Western country.

The Nammadā and the Vāṇijagāma of the Burmese do not fulfil any of these conditions. Their Sunāparanta or Aparanta is not to the West, but, according to Buddhist cosmology, to the East; their Nammadā is not a river flowing into the sea, but an insignificant hill steam flowing into a river; their Vāṇijagāma therefore cannot, in any possible manner, be a seaport. The author or authors of the Samôn have so well understood this that they make Cuḷapuṇṇa embark at Negrais Island, in order to give to their falsification a plausible appearance of truth. As to the mountain "Makuḷa" or "Mātula," it is with more common sense placed in India by the *Mónrājavan*.[4]

(1) Cf. Burnouf, *Introduction*, page 252 (or 225), note 2, where he says that Wilford, taking his information from the *Varāhasamhitā*, speaks of Aparāntikās situated to the west.

(2) McCrindle, *Ancient India as described by Ptolemy*, and Yule, *Hobson-Jobson*, *s.v.* Supāra.

(3) McCrindle, *ibid.*

(4) Rangoon, 1899, page 75.

However, the names of Sunāparanta and Aparanta [1] having been given to a Burmese province, it became necessary to cite authoritative texts in order, if possible, to legalize, so to say, this plagiarism by means of the sacred books. And this, the Burmese have done, but very clumsily, for their favourite text goes directly against their assertion. The *Sāsanālankāra*[2] enumerating the names of the missionaries who, according to the *Dipavamsa* [3] were sent to different countries during the eighteenth year of Asoka's reign, and also the names of those countries, says that that *bhikkhu Yonarakkhita* was sent to Aparanta (Aparāntaka) and adds that Aparāntaka is the same as Sunāparanta in Burma. As a conclusive proof of this identity he (the author of the Sāsanāla*n*kāra) gives [4] the story of the Sakka (Sanskrit Çakra) Mandhātā: Mandhātā had brought with him to the *devaloka* an inhabitant from each of three of the four great islands or continents (mahādipa); these three unfortunate men being unable, for a very simple reason (they did not know the way, and the Sakka was dead), to go back to their homes, approached the *parināyakaratana*, *viz.*, the Sakka's eldest son, who assigned to each of them a country corresponding, by its position at least, to the one he had left: Videha, being to the East, would, in future, be the country of the inhabitant of Pubbavideha, the Eastern island; Kuru, in the North, would become that of the citizen of the Northern Island, Uttarakuru; and the inhabitant of Aparagoyānadipa, the Western Island, would have for his country Aparanta, the West-country.[5] The Sāsanāla*n*kāra here, adds—" and as the son (sūna) of Sakka assigned to him this country to live in in future, Aparanta is also called Sunāparanta, " the West Country of

(1) See *Inscriptions collected by King Bodawpaya*, Vol. I, page 19, line 12; *ibid*, page 43, line 5, and in many other places. *Cf.* Vohāralina*tth*adipani, page 221: " Sunāparanta, which includes: Caku, Cala*n*, Bo*n*-la*n*, Lê-kô*n*, So*n*-svap, etc.; Tampadipa, which includes: Sārekhettara, Pagan, Pa*n*-ya, etc."

(2) Rangoon, 1897, page 22.

(3) Chapter VIII; also *Mahâvamsa*, Chapter XII.

(4) The author of the *Sāsanālankāra*, generally so accurate in his quotations, says that this story is found in the commentary on the *Mahâsatipa*tthā*nasutta* (*Dīghanikāya*, *Mahâvagga*, IX); it is not so: the story is in the commentary on the Mahānidānasutta (*ibid.*, II).

(5) *Mahanidānasutta*tth*akathā*.

Sakka's son; Sunāparanta or Aparanta is then, incontestably, in Burma (!)" Such is, in fact, the often recurring etymology given by the Burmese to this word: but the text is most flagrantly violated, for it shows clearly that the Commentators place Aparanta, *alias* Sunāparanta, to the West and not to the East, as the Burmese will at any cost have it.

From what has above been said it may be gathered: (*a*) That the Burmese, before the eleventh century and the beginning of the twelfth, do not seem to have known the bank of the Irrawaddy, behind and above Pagan, under the name of Aparanta or Sunāparanta. Pagan itself was included in the province of Tampadipa.[1] The inscriptions of that period do not mention this name (at least, as far as I have been able to verify this assertion by means of the inscriptions already published), and it is remarkable that the *Mahārājavan* in the long notice consecrated to Anorata, does not introduce this name, as also does the *Paganrājavan*[2] which places Saku, Lêkô*n*, Sô*n*svap, etc. (towns always enumerated as being in Sunāparanta) in Pūrantappa, a name which is now forgotten and appears to be the original name of the province later known as Sunāparanta.

(*b*) That the form "Sonāparanta" is not known in Burma, though always given by Yule, the form Sunāparanta being always found in the inscriptions and in documents; no Burmese authority anywhere gives to this word the meaning of the Aurea Regio of Ptolemy, and, if the ancients knew this part of Burma under this appellation, it seems to have been unknown by the Burmese themselves, who, after having borrowed it, under another form, from the Pāli A*tth*akathās, do not understand it as meaning "golden frontier."

(*c*) In the A*tth*akathās, Aparanta or Sunāparanta does not designate Central Burma, but a country situated to the West, on the sea-shore, possessing a famous seaport at the estuary of the river Nammadā (Narmadā, Nerbudda). Now, Aparanta has been identified with the Konkan; Sūrpākara, the great trading centre

(1) *Cf. supra*, page 13, note 1.

(2) The *Paganrājavan* uses the word "Sunāparanta" in the history of the reign of King Sen Lan Kro*n*; but the *Paganrājavan* was compiled many centuries after the fall of Pagan, and at a time when this name was popular and known to everybody; it must, therefore, not be inferred from this that the name already existed in the time of Sen Lan Kro*n*.

of Western India, with Supāra and the Narmadā with the Nerbudda; moreover, the Commentary on the *Dīghanikāya* locates Aparanta, most expressly to the west.

The Burmese, then have renamed, from a Pāli legend, a province, a torrent and a small town of the Valley of the Irrawaddy and, to justify themselves in doing so, have deliberately voilated two texts which are most explicit and plain.

## EXTRACT FROM THE PU*NN*OVADASUTTA*TTH*AKATHA.

### TEXT.(1)

"Atha kho āyasmā Pu*nn*o'ti..." Ko pan'esa Pu*nn*o? Kasmā ca pan'ettha gantukāmo ahositi? Sunāparantavāsiko [2] eva esa, Sāvatthiya*m* pana asappāya*m* vihāra*m* sallakkhetvā, tattha gantukāmo ahosi. Tatrāya*m* anupubbikathā.

Sunāparantara*t*t*h*e kira ekasmi*m* vā*n*ijagāme ete dve bhātaro; tesu kadāci je*t*t*h*o pa*n*casaka*t*asatāni gahetvā janapada*m* gantvā bha*nd*a*m* āharati, kadāci kani*tth*o. Imasmi*m* pana samaye kani*t*-*t*ha*m* ghare *th*apetvā je*tth*abhātiko pa*n*casaka*t*asatāni gahetvā, janapadacārika*m* caranto anupubbena Sāvatthi*m* patvā Jetavanassa nātidūre saka*t*asattha*m* nivāsetvā, bhuttapātarāso parijanaparivuto phāsuka*tt*h*ā*ne [3] nisīdi. Tena ca samayena Sāvatthivāsino bhuttapātarāsā uposatha*n*gāni adhi*tth*āya suddhuttarāsa*n*gā gandhapupphā [4] dihatthā yena Buddho yena Dhammo yena Sa*n*gho tanninnā tappo*n*ā tappabbhārā hutvā, dakkhi [5] *n*advārena nikkhamitvā Jetavana*m* gacchanti So te disvā "kaha*m* [6] ime gacchantīti" eka*m* manussa*m* [7] pucchi. "Kin tva*m* ayyo na jānāsi loke Buddhadhammasa*n*gharatanāni [8] nāma uppannāni icceso mahājano Satthu santika*m* dhammakatha*m* sotu*m* gacchatīti." Tassa Buddho'ti vacana*m* chavicammādīni chinditvā a*tth*imiñja*m* āhacca a*tth*āsi. Attano parijanaparivuto [9] tāya [10] parisāya saddhi*m* vihāra*m*

(1) I had at my disposal, to establish the text, two manuscripts. The first, *B*, very defective, is in the Bernard Free Library, Rangoon; the text is full of corrections and mistakes; the second, *A*, much more correct, was lent to me by the abbot of the Mezali monastery, Rangoon; it is written very legibly and contains but few mistakes. I, therefore, took it as a basis, merely noting the principal mistakes of *B*. A third manuscript was sent to me when the work was finished; but it is still more defective than *B*, of which it reproduces the majority of the mistakes; I did not, on that account, think it necessary to use it; it appears, moreover, to have been copied from *B*. (2) *A* Sunāparantare. (3) *B* bāsuka (4) *B* puppa .. (5) *B* dakkha*n*a.... (6) *B* kata*m*. (7) *B* manussa. (8) *A*... ratanāna*m*. (9) *A* parivato. (10) *B* parijanaparivutāya parisāya.

ga*n*tvā Satthu madhurasarena dhamma*m* [1] desentassa [2] parisapariyante *th*ito dhamma*m* [3] sutvā pabbajjāya [4] citta*m* [5] uppādesi. Atha Tathāgatena kāla*m* viditvā parisāya [6] uyyojitāya Satthāra*m* upasa*n*kamitvā vanditvā svātanāya nimantetvā, dutiyadivase ma*nd*apa*m* kāretvā āsanāni paññāpetvā Buddhapamukhassa sa*n*ghassa mahādāna*m* datvā, bhuttapātarāso uposatha*n*gāni [7] adhi*tth*āya bha*nd*āgārika*m* pakkosāpetvā: " Ettaka*m* dhana*m* [8] vissajjita*m*, ettaka*m* na [9] vissajjitan ti " sabba*m* ācikkhitvā, "ima*m* sāpateyya*m* mayha*m* [10] kani*tth*assa dehīti" sabba*m* niyyādetvā, Satthu santike pabbajitvā [11] kamma*tth*ānaparāyano ahosi. Ath'assa kamma*tth*āna*m* manasikarontassa kamma*tth*āna*m* na upa*tth*āti; tato cintesi: " Aya*m* janapado mayha*m* asappāyo [12], yannūnāha*m* Satthu santike kamma*tth*āna*m* gahetvā saka*ratth*a*m* eva gaccheyyan ti." Atha pubba*n*hasamaye [13] pi*nd*āya caritvā sāya*n*he [14] pa*t*isallā*n*ā [15] vu*tth*ahitvā Bhagavanta*m* upasa*n*kamitvā kamma*tth*āna*m* kathāpetvā sattasīhanāde [16] naditvā pakkāmi. Tena vutta*m*: " Atha kho āyasmā Pu*nn*o — pa — viharatīti. [17]" Kattha panāya*m* vihāsīti? Catūsu *th*ānesu vihāsi. Sunāparantara*tth*a*m* tāva pavisitvā ca Appahatapabbata*m* nāma pavisitvā Vā*n*ijagāma*m* pi*nd*āya pāvisi Atha na*m* kani*tth*abhātā sañjānitvā bhikkha*m* datvā: " Bhante, aññattha agantvā idh'eva [18] vasathāti " pa*t*iñña*m* kāretvā tatth'eva vasāpesi. Tato Samuddagirivihāra*m* nāma agamāsi; tattha ayakantapāsā*n*ehi paricchinditvā katacaṅkamo atthi; ta*m* koci ca*n*kamitu*m* samattho nāma n'atthi; tattha samuddavīciyo [19] āgantvā [20] ayakantapāsā*n*esu paharitvā mahāsadda*m* karonti. Thero: " Kamma*tth*āna*m* manasikarontāna*m* phāsuvihāro hotūti " samudda*m* nisadda*m* katvā adhi*tth*āsi. Tato Mātulagiri*m* nāma agamāsi; tattha pi saku*n*asa*n*gho ussanno [21] rattiñ ca divā ca saddo eko bandho [22] va ahosi; thero: "Ida*m* *th*āna*m* na phāsukan ti" tato Paku*l*a [23] kārāmavihāra*m* nāma gato; so Vā*n*ijagāmassa nātiduro naccāsanno gamanāgamanasampanno vivitto appa-

([1]) *B* dhamma. ([2]) *B* desentassa*m*. ([3]) *B* dhamma. ([4]) *A* and *B* pappaj... ([5]) *A* and *B* citta. ([6]) *B* pariyāya. ([7]) *B*. thagāni. ([8]) *A has* pana *and omits* dhanam. ([9]) *B has* pana *before* na. ([10]) *A omits* mayha*m*. ([11]) *B* pappaj ([12]) A appāyo. ([13]) *B* pubbanasamaye. ([14]) *B* Sayanhe. ([15]) *A*... sallānā. ([16]) *B* Satthusīhanānaditvā. ([17]) *see text of the* Saññuttanikāya, Sa*l*ayatana, Pu*nn*ovādasutta ed. Feer, Volume IV, page 63. ([18]) *B* icceva. ([19]) *A* viciyo; *B*...gijaciyo. ([20]) *A* agantvā. ([21]) *B* ussano. ([22] bhan to. ([23]) B Paku*lh*a (?)

saddo; thero: "Ima*m* *th*āna*m* phāsukan ti" tattha ratti*tth*ānadivā*th*ānaca*n*kamanādīni kāretvā vāsa*m* upagacchi. Eva*m* catūsu *th*ānesu vihāsi.

Ath'ekadivasa*m* tasmi*m* yeva antovasse pañcavā*n*ijakasatāni [1]: "Pārasamudda*m* gacchāmāti" nāvāya bha*nd*a*m* pakkhipi*m*su. Nāvārohanadivase therassa kani*tth*abhātā thera*m* bhojetvā therassa santike sikkhāpadāni gahetvā vanditvā: "Bhante, samuddo nāma asaddheyo [2] anekantarāyo āvajjeyyāthāti" vatvā nāva*m* āruhi. Nāvā uttamajavena [3] gacchamānā aññatara*m* dīpaka*m* pāpu*n*i; manussā: "Pātarāsa*m* karissāmāti" dīpake utti*nn*ā. Tasmi*m* pana dīpake aññа*m* kiñci n'atthi, candanavana*m* eva ahosi. Ath'eko vāsiyā rukkha*m* āko*t*etvā lohitacandanabhāva*m* ñatvā āha: "Bho! maya*m* lābhatthāya pārasamudda*m* gacchāma, ito ca uttari*m* lābho nāma n'atthi, catura*n*gulamattā [4] gha*t*ikā satasahassa*m* agghati. hāretabbayuttaka*m* bha*nd*a*m* hāretvā candanassa pūremāti. [5]" Te tathā kari*m*su. Candanavane adhivattthā [6] amanussā kujjhitvā: "Imehi amhāka*m* candanavana*m* nāsita*m* ghā*t*essāma [7] ne 'ti" cintetvā, "idh'eva ghā*t*itesu sabba*m* ekaku*n*apa*m* bhavissati samuddamajjhe nesa*m* nāva*m* osīdāpessāmāti [8]" āha*m*su. Atha tesa*m* nāva*m* āruyha muhutta*m* gatakāle yeva uppā*t*ika*m* [9] u*tth*āpetvā saya*m* pi te amanussā bhayānakāni rūpāni dassayi*m*su. Bhītā manussā attano attano devatāna*m* namassanti. Therassa kani*tth*o Culapu*nn*o ku*t*umbiko [10]: Mayha*m* bhātā avassayo hotūti" therassa nāma*m* saramāno a*tth*āsi. Thero pi kira tasmi*m* yeva kha*n*e āvajjitva [11] tesa*m* byasanappati*m* ñatvā vehāsa*m* uppatitvā abhimukho a*tth*āsi. Amanussā thera*m* disvā va apakkami*m*su [12], uppā*t*ika*m* sannisīdi. Thero: "Mā bhāyathāti" te assāsetvā, "kaha*m* gantukām'atthāti" pucchi. "Bhante, amhāka*m* saka*tth*āna*m* eva gacchissāmāti. [13]" "Thero nāva*n*ga*n*e akkamitvā: [14] "Etesa*m* icchita*tth*āna*m* gacchatūti" adhi*tth*āsi. Vā*n*ijā saka*tth*āna*m* gantvā ta*m* pavatti*m* puttadārassa ārocetvā: "Etha, thera*m* sara*n*a*m* gacchāmāti" pañcasatā pi attano pañcahi mātugāmasatehi saddhi*m* tīsu sara*n*esu pati*tth*āya upāsakatta*m* pa*t*ivedesu*m*. Tato nāvāya bha*nd*a*m* otāretvā therass'eka*m* ko*tth*āsa*m* [15] katvā: "Aya*m*, bhante, tumhāka*m*

(1) *B* pā*n*ija... (2) B asaddvejo... (3) *B* utta pajagavana (!). (4) *B* caturagula. (5) *B* pūrethāti. (6) *A* .. vatto. (7) *A* ghātes .. (8) *A and B* osīdissāmāti. (9) *A* uppādik... (10) *A* ku*t*umpiko. (11) *B* bhāv... (12) *B* pakk... (13) *A* gacchāmāti. (14) *B* nāvaga*n*e attametvā. (15) *B* ka*tth*akam.

ko*tth*āso ti" āha*m*su. Thero: "Mayha*m* visu*m* ko*tth*āsakiccam n'atthi: Satthā pana tumhehi di*tth*apubbo'ti?"—"Na di*tth*apubbo, bhante'ti." — "Tena hi, iminā Satthu ma*nd*alamā*l*a*m* karotha, eva*m* Satthāra*m* passissathāti." Te "Sādhu, bhante'ti" tena ca ko*tth*āsena attano ca ko*tth*āsehi ma*nd*alamāla*m* kāretu*m* ārabhi*m*su. Satthā pi kira āraddhakālato pa*tth*āya paribhoga*m* akāsi. Ārakkhamanussā ratti*m* obhāsa*m* disvā: "Mahesakkhā devatā atthīti" sañña*m* [1] kari*m*su. Upāsakā ma*nd*a*l*amālañ ca bhikkhusa*n*ghassa ca āsanāni ni*tth*āpetvā dānasambhāra*m* sajjetva: "Kata*m*, bhante, amhehi attano kicca*m*, Satthāra*m* pakkosathāti" therassa ārocesu*m*. Thero sāya*n*hasamaye iddhiyā Sāvatthi*m* gantvā: "Bhante, Vā*n*ijagāmavāsino tumhe da*tth*ukāmā, tesa*m* anukampa*m* karothāti" Bhagavanta*m* yāci. Bhagavā adhivāsesi; thero saka*tth*āna*m* eva paccāgato. Bhagavā pi Ānandathera*m* āmantesi: "Ānanda, sve [2] Sunāparante Vā*n*ijagāme pi*nd*āya carissāma; tva*m* ekūnapa*n*casatāna*m* bhikkhūna*m* salāka*m* dehīti." Thero: "Sādhu, bhante'ti" bhikkhusa*n*ghassa ta*m* attha*m* ārocetvāna [3] va: "cārikabhikkhū salāka*m* ga*n*hantūti" āha. Ta*m* divasa*m* Ku*nd*odhānathero pa*th*ama*m* salāka*m* aggahesi. Vā*n*ijagāmavāsino pi: "Sve kira Satthā āgamissati" gāmamajjhe ma*nd*apa*m* katvā dānagga*m* sajjayi*m*su. Bhagavā pāto va sarīrapa*t*ijaggana*m* katvā gandhaku*t*i*m* pavisitvā phalasamāpatti*m* appetvā nisīdi. Sakkassa pa*nd*ukambalasilāsana*m* [4] u*n*ha*m* ahosi. So: "Ki*m* idan ti" āvajjetvā Satthu Sunāparantagamana*m* disvā Visukamma*m* āmantesi: "Tāta, ajja Bhagavā ti*m*samattāni yojanasatāni pi*nd*acārika*m* gamissati; pañcaku*t*āgārasatāni māpetvā Jetavanadvārako*tth*akamatthake gamanasajjāni katvā *th*apehī ti." [5] So tathā akāsi. Bhagavato ku*t*āgāra*m* catumukha*m* ahosi, dvinna*m* aggasāvakāna*m* dvimukhāni, sesāni ekamukhāni. Satthā gandhaku*t*ito nikkhamma pa*t*ipā*t*iyā thapitaku*t*āgaresu varaku*t*āgāram pāvisi; dve aggasāvake ādi*m* katvā ekunapañcabhikkhhusatāni pi pañca [6] ku*t*āgārasatāni ahesu*m*, eka*m* tuccha*m* ku*t*āgāra*m* ahosi; pañcaku*t*āgārasatāni ākāse uppati*m*su. Satthā Saccabandhapabbata*m* nāma patvā ku*t*āgāra*m* ākāse *th*apesi. Tasmi*m* pabbate Saccabandho nāma micchādi*tth*ikatāpaso mahājana*m* micchādi*tth*i*m* ugga*n*hāpento lābhaggayasaggapatto hutvā vasati. Abbhantare c' assa antocā*t*iya*m* padīpo viya arahattaphalassa

(1) Aññām. (2) *A* se. (3) *B* ārocetvā navatarikabhikkhu... ga*n*hantūti.
(4) ...*B* silāsana*m*.
(5) *B*. thapetīti. (6) The two *Mss.* omit pañca.

upanissayo jalati. Ta*m* disvā: "Dhamma*m* assa [1] kathessāmīti" gantvā dhamma*m* [2] desesi; tāpaso desanāpariyosāne arahatta*m* pāpu*n*i, maggen'ev'assa abhinnā āgatā, ehibhikkhu hutvā iddhimayapattacīvaradharo ku*t*āgāra*m* pāvisi. Bhagavā ku*t*āgāragatehi pañcahi bhikkhusatehi saddhi*m* Vā*n*ijagāma*m* gantvā ku*t*āgārāni adissamānakāni katvā Vā*n*ijagāma*m* pāvisi. Vā*n*ijā Buddhapamukhassa sa*n*ghassa mahādāna*m* datvā Satthāra*m* Maku*l*akārāma*m* nayi*m*su; Satthā ma*nd*alamāla*m* pāvisi. Mahājano: "Yāva Satthā [3] gattadaratha*m* pa*t*ippassambhetīti [4]" pātarāsa*m* gantvā uposatha*n*gāni samādāya bahu*m* gandhañ ca pupphañ ca ādāya dhammasavanatthāya ārāma*m* agamāsi; Satthā dhamma*m* desesi, mahājanassa bandhanā mokkho jāto; mahanta*m* Buddhakolāhala*m* [5] ahosi. Satthā mahājanassa sa*n*gahattha*m* [6] sattāha*m* tatth'eva vasi; aru*n*a*m* pana mahāgandhaku*t*iya*m* u*tt*hāpesi. Sattāha*m* pi dhammadesanāpariyosāne caturāsitiyā pā*n*asahassāna*m* dhammābhisamayo ahosi. Tattha sattāha*m* [7] vasitvā Vā*n*ijagāme pi*nd*āya caritvā: "Tva*m* idh'eva vasāhīti" Pu*n*natthera*m* nivattetvā, antare Nammadānadī [8] nāma atthi, tassa tīra*m* agamāsi. Nammadānāgarājā [9] Satthu paccuggamana*m* katvā nāgabhavana*m* pavesetvā ti*n*na*m* ratanāna*m* sakkāra*m* akāsi. Satthā tassa dhamma*m* kathetvā nāgabhavanā nikkhami [10]; so: "Mayha*m*, bhante, paricaritabba*m* dethāti" yāci. Bhagavā Nammadānadītīre padacetiya*m* dassesi; ta*m* vicīsu āgatāsu pidhīyati [11] gatāsu vivarīyati mahāsakkārappatta*m* ahosi. Satthā tato nikkhamitvā Saccabandhapabbata*m* gantvā Saccabandha*m* āha: "Tayā mahājano apāyamagge otārito [12], tva*m* idh'eva vasitvā etesa*m* laddhi*m* [13] visajjāpetvā nibbānamagge pati*tt*hāpehīti." So'pi paricaritabba*m* yāci. Satthā ghana [14] pi*tt*hipāsā*n*e allamattika [15] pi*nd*imhi [16] lañchana*m* viya padacetiya*m* dassesi. Tato Jetavana*m* eva gato. Eta*m* attha*m* sandhāya: "Ten'evantaravassen'ādi" [17] vutta*m*. (Parinibbāyīti anupādhisesāya nibbānadhātuyā parinibbāyi) [18]. Mahājano therassa sattadivasāni sarīrapūja*m* katvā bahūni gandhaka*tt*hāni samodhānetvā sarīra*m* jhāpetvā dhātuyo ādāya cetiya*m* akāsi.

(1) *B* dhommassa. (2) *B omits* dhamma*n*. (3) *B* sattā. (4) *A* pa*t*ipas... (5) *B*... kolā ala*m*. (6) *B* sa*n*gāh... (7) *B* satth'āha*m*. (8) *B* Nammadānanadī. (9) *B* Nammadānanāgarājā. (10) *B* Nnikkhama*m*. (11) *B* viyatī. (12) *A* otarito. (13) *B* laddha*m*. (14) *A* ghānap .. (15) *B*... patti. (16) *B*... pi*nd*amhi.

(17) See the text of the Pu*nn*ovādasutta, *loc. laud.* (18) This belongs to the commentary on the *sutta*.

## TRANSLATION.

"*At that time,*[1] are we told, the *reverend Punna* . . . ." But who was this Pu*n*na? and why was he desirous to go there? [2] He was a native of Sunāparanta and perceiving that the sojourn of Savatthi was not suitable [3] to him, he wished to go back to his country. Here is the regular story.

In a certain merchants' village [4] in the kingdom of Sunāparanta there lived *these* two brothers. [5] Sometimes the elder, taking five hundred carts, would go to the districts and bring goods; at other times the younger one would go. Now on this occasion, the elder brother left the younger one at home, took five hundred carts and went from district to district so that in time he reached Savatthi, and made his caravan encamp not far from the Jetavana. Then having breakfasted, he sat down, surrounded by his retinue, in an agreeable spot. At this moment, the citizens of Sāvatthi, after their morning meal, having resolved to observe the *Uposatha* precepts were leaving the town by the southern gate and going to the Jetavana clad all in white, carrying perfumes, flowers and so forth, attracted by an invincible inclination towards the Buddha, the Doctrine and the assembly of the Brethren. Pu*n*na saw them, and asked one of them: "Whither are these going?" "What! Sir, dost not thou know that the Three Jewels—the Buddha, the Doctrine, and the Assembly of the Brethen—have appeared in the world? These people are going to the Buddha to hear him preach the Law." The word "Buddha" thrilled [6] him. Surrounded by his retinue he repaired to the monastery with the congregation and standing behind them, listened to the master preaching the doctrine ni a sweet voice; having heard the doctrine he conceived a desire for the religious life. When the Tathāgata, knowing the moment was come, had sent back the assembly, Pu*n*na approached the master and having

(1) In the Saññyutta-nikāya (*cf.* ed. Feer, Vol. IV, page 60).

(2) That is, to Sunāparanta.

(3) For the exercise of Kammat*th*āna, or religious meditation.

(4) Vā*n*ijagāma, might also be translated as a proper noun: Hardy, *Manual of Buddhism*, page 260, translates this word by "the merchant's village."

(5) That is, Mahāpu*n*na, the elder and the hero of the story, and his brother Cūlapu*n*na *cf.* page 1.

(6) Lit., "pierced his skin and penetrated to the marrow of his bones."

saluted him, invited him for the morrow. On the next day, he had a pavilion built wherein he prepared seats, and gave great offerings to the clergy with Buddha at their head; then, himself having finished his morning meal, bound himself to observe the eight precepts. He then called his treasurer: "So much has been spent, so much has not been," and he gave him the account of everything; "Give this property to my younger brother"; and he made over everything to him, after which, he received ordination at the master's hands and lost himself in meditation. But although he devoted himself to it, he did not succeed: then, he thought, "This country is not favourable to me; what if I were to ask for a subject for meditation from the Master and go back to my country?" He made his morning tour for food, and, in the evening, rising from his seclusion, approached the Blessed One and having made him recite a formula for meditation, uttered seven joyful exclamations and departed. It is why it is said: "*At that time the reverend Punna* . . . . dwelt." But where did he dwell? He dwelt in four places. He first entered the kingdom of Sunāparanta, went to the Appahata mountain, and entered into the merchants' village (Vā*n*ijagāma) for his food. His brother recognized him, fed him and told him: "Reverend, do not go anywhere else, but dwell even here," and having made him promise to do so, he put him up in that place. Thence, he went to the Samuddagiri (the ocean mountain) monastery, where there was a cloistered walk marked out by lodestones;[1] but nobody could walk therein (to meditate), for the billows, breaking on those stones, made a great noise. The *thera* said: "Let this be a pleasant spot for those given up to meditation" and, by the power of his resolution, he made the ocean quiet. Thence he repaired to the Mātula mountain; but there, too, were flocks of birds, making a perpetual noise, night and day; the *thera* thought: "This spot is not suitable," and he went to the monastery of Paku*l*aka. This monastery was neither far from nor near the merchants' village; it was in a retired spot, quiet, and communications were easy. The *thera*, thinking: "This is a suitable place," had built therein for himself a cell for the night and one for the day, a covered walk, etc., and

(1) *Cf.* Hardy, *Manual of Buddhism*, page 260; to these places he gives the names of Mudugiri, Mailigiri and Muluarāma.

dwelt there. Thus he lived in four places. [1] Then, one day, in that very period of *vassa*, five hundred traders, intending to cross the ocean, loaded a ship with goods. On the day of embarking the *thera's* younger brother, having fed the latter and received from him the precepts, [2] saluted him : " The ocean, your reverence, is not to be trusted ; it is full of dangers ; you should think (of us)." Having thus spoken he went on board. The ship, going with great speed, came to a certain island : " Let us prepare breakfast," said the men and they disembarded on the island. Now, on that island, there was nothing but a forest of sandal ; one of the traders, having struck a tree with an axe and perceiving it was red sandal, said : " Friends ! we cross the seas for the sake of gain ; now, there is no greater gain then from this, a bit about four inches [3] is worth one hundred thousand (coins). Let us get rid of all the goods we can and let us make a full cargo of sandalwood." So they did. The goblins [4] inhabiting the sandal forest were enraged : " Our sandal forest has been destroyed by these people, let us kill them !" said they ; but they reflected : " If we kill them here, the whole island will become a charnel house ; let us sink their vessel in mid-ocean." The traders re-embarked ; but after a few moments, the goblins caused a storm to rise and shewed themselves to them under fearful shapes. Terrified, the men worshipped each his tutelary deity. The *thera's* brother, Cû*l*apu*nn*a the householder, thought : " Let my brother be my refuge !" and he mentally invoked the *thera's* name. At this very moment, the *thera*, thinking (of the merchants) perceived they were near their ruin ; he rose into the sky and stood before them. The goblins seeing him, fled. " Do not fear," said the *thera* to the traders, and having comforted them,

(1) The whole story, from beginning to end, occupies but one season of *vassa* or "rainy season." Mahāpu*nn*a was looking out for a suitable spot, wherein to spend, in quiet, the lenten season, as is practised even now-a-days, and retired at last near Vā*n*ijagâma (the Lê-kô*n* လယ်ကုန်း , of the Burmese).

(2) It must be understood that he promises the Thera to observe the five moral precepts or *sila*, which are binding on all good Buddhists.

(3) Burnouf, *Introduction* (page 258 or 230), speaks of a Tibetan measure called *pho* : the Burmese have also a weight, now become obsclete, called *po* and equal to five ticals ; it is mentioned in the Burmese version of the *Vessantarajātaka*.

(4) a-manussā = non-men.

he enquired whither they desired to go; they answered: "Reverend Sir, we wish to go to our country." The *thera* came on deck and formed the mental resolution—"Let this ship go where they desire!" The merchants, having gone back to their country, told these events to their families: "Come," said they, "let us take our refuge in the *thera*, [1] " and the five hundred merchants, with their five hundred wives, having been established in the Three Refuges, [2] announced they were (now) lay disciples. They then unloaded the vessel, and offered one share (of the sandal cargo) to the *thera*, saying, "Reverend Sir, here is your share." But he answered, "I have personally no need of a share. But, have you ever seen the Master?" "No, Reverend Sir, we have never seen him." "Very well, then, with this share build a pavilion, [3] and thus, you will see the Master." "Very well, Reverend," said they, and with his share and theirs they began building the pavilion. It is said that, from the time they began to build, the Master took possession of it. The watchmen, seeing in the night a light, thought that a powerful god lived there. The lay disciples having finished the building, arranged seats for the clergy and prepared the things intended as offerings, apprized the *thera* that their task was over and that he should invite the Master. Early in the morning, the *thera*([4]) went to Savatthi by means of his superhuman power and begged of the Blessed One: "Lord, the inhabitants of Vā*n*ijagāma are desirous to see you; do them this favour." The Blessed One consented, and the *thera* came back, and the Blessed One called the *thera* Ànandā: "Ànandā," said he, "to-morrow, we shall go to Vā*n*ijagāma in Sunāparanta, for our food, give out tickets to 499 monks." The *thera* said: "Even so, Lord"; and, having told that matter to the assembled monks, he invited those that had to come to take their ticket. On that day, the *thera* Ku*nd*odhāna took out the first ticket. [5] The inhabitants of Vā*n*ijagāma, knowing the Master would come on the morrow, built a

([1]) That is, "Let us become Buddhists and the Thera's disciples."

([2]) The Buddha, his Doctrine and the Order.

([3]) The *samôn* says: a monastery. It is supposed still to exist under the name of Na*n*-sā-kro*n* ( နံ့သာကျောင်း ), "the sandal monastery."

([4]) Hardy, *Manual of Buddhism*, page 209, translates: "the priest Sunāparanta," instead of: "the priest of Sunāparanta."

([5]) Mere allusion to an incident which is told *in extenso* in the *Divyāvadāna*. Burnouf, *Introduction* (page 260 or 237, note 1), tries to find the etymology of

shed in the middle of the village and prepared a hall for the offerings. The Blessed One, having finished his ablutions early in the morning, entered his room (lit., the Perfumed Chamber) and sat, meditating deeply on the fruition of the Path. The marble throne of Sakka (Sanskrit Çakra) became hot. Sakka considered what the cause was, and, seeing the Master was about to go to Sunāparanta, he called Visukamma (Sanskrit Viçvakarman): "Dear son, to-day, the Blessed One will go on a begging tour of thirty and one hundred *yojanas*: make five hundred kiosks and place them, ready to go, on the portico of the Jetavana. Visukamma did so. The kiosk of the Blessed One had four entrances, those of the two principal disciples [1] had two, and the rest one entrance each. The Master left his room, and, among the kiosks ranged in a line, entered the most magnificent. Counting the two principal disciples, there were four hundred and ninty-nine monks and five hundred kiosks, of which one was empty. The five hundred kiosks rose into the sky. When the Master arrived at the mountain called Saccabandha, he stopped his kiosk in the air. On this mountain lived a religious heretic, known as Saccabandha, who taught

the name: Ku*nd*opadhāna; it will be remarked that the pāli text calls this monk simply: Ku*nd*odhāna. He is also mentioned (Eka*n*guttara, Etadaggavaggo) as being one of the eighty princpal disciples of the Buddha, and the commentary on the Eka*n*guttara gives, to explain his name, this amusing story. In a previous existence he had been a Bhūma-devatā and committed certain faults, the fruits of which he reaped in his subsequent states of existence; the commentary goes on:

"Bhumadevatā tassa kammassa nissandena eka*m* buddhantara*m* apāyato na muccittha; sace pana kālena kāla*m* manussatta*m* āgacchati aññena kenaci kato doso tass'eva upari patati. Eso amhāka*m* Bhagavato kāle Sāva*tth*iya*m* brāhma*n*akule nibbatti; Dhānamā*n*avo'ti tassa nāma*m* aka*m*su. So vayappatto tayo bede ugga*n*hitvā mahallakakāle Satthu dhammadesana*m* sutvā pa*t*iladdhasaddho pabbajitvā tassa upasa*m*pannadivasato pa*tth*āya ekā ala*n*katapa*t*iyat*t*ā itthi, tasmi*m* gāma*m* pavisante tena saddhi*m* eva gāma*m* pavisati, nikkhamante nikkhamati, vihāra*m* pavisante pi pavisatīti, ti*tth*ante pi ti*tth*ati. Eva*m* niccānubandhā paññāyati. Thero ta*m* pana passati, tassa pana purimassa kammassa nissandena upa*tth*itvā (?) gāme yāgubhikkha*m* dadamānā itthiyo: 'Bhante, aya*m* eko yāgu u*lu*n*ko tumhāka*m*, eko imissā amhāka*m* sahāyikāyā'ti' parihāsa*m* karonti. Therassa mahatī vihesā hoti; vihāragata*m* pi sāma*n*erā c'eva harabhikkhū ca parivāretvā: 'Dhāno ko*nd*o jāto'ti' parihāsa*m* karonti. Ath' assa ten'eva kāra*n*ena ko*nd*odhānathero'ti nāma*m* jāta*m*."

(1) Moggallāna and Sāriputta.

heretical doctrines to the people; he enjoyed the best offerings and the greatest honours; but in his heart, like a lamp hidden in a vase, shone his predestination to sanctity. Seeing this (the Buddha thought): "I will expound the Doctrine to him" and going, preached a sermon to him. The monk, at the end of this religious instruction, became a saint, and in the way, [1] obtained the six supernatural faculties, and then, having became a monk according to the formula, [2] "Ehi bikkhu," he suddenly found himself carrying an alms-bowl and wearing robes created by the miraculous power of the Buddha; and he entered into the kiosk. [3] Then, the Blessed One with the five hundred monks in their kiosks, went towards the merchants' village (Vā*n*ijagāma), and having made the kiosks invisible, entered the village. The merchants, having given great offerings to the clergy with the Buddha at their head, took the Master to the Makula Monastery, and the Master entered into the pavilion. The people said: "Meanwhile, let the Master rest himself from his bodily fatigue," and they went to their breakfast; then, they took upon themselves the performance of the precepts and, loaded with perfumes and flowers, went to the monastery to listen to the Law. The Master expounded his Doctrine, and the people were freed from their bonds; and there was a great uproar caused by the Buddha's presence.

The master dwelt there for a week, for the people's spiritual benefit, sitting up in the "Perfumed Chamber" [4] till the break of day. At the close of these seven days' preaching, 84,000 persons attained to the understanding of the Law. Having (then) dwelt there for a week, he entered Vā*n*ijagāma on his begging tour, and, assigning it to the *Thera* Pu*nn*a for his residence, left him. On the way there was a river called Nammadā; he went to the bank thereof. The king of the Nammadā Nāgas came forth to meet the master, took him into the Nāga-mansion and did honour to the Three Jewels. The Master unfolded to him the Doctrine and left his abode, and the Nāga king begged of him: "Lord, give me

(1) That is, while he was advancing towards the Buddha.

(2) "*Ehi, bhikkhu!* Come, O mendicant!" This was the usual formula with which the Buddha received in his Order, the persons desirous of leading the religious life.

(3) The kiosk which had been kept empty.

(4) Thus was called his private room

something that I may honour." [1] The Blessed One impressed [2] and left as a relic the mark of his foot on the bank of the river Nammadā. This imprint was covered by the waves at the time of high water, and uncovered when the water subsided, and it was greatly venerated. The Master left this spot, went to the Saccabandha mountain and said to Saccabandha: "Through thee, the people have entered on the way to perdition; stay here, make them reject these false notions and establish them in the way to Nirvā*n*a." He, too, asked of the Master something which he might revere. The Master imprinted the mark of his foot on the solid, flat rock as easily as he would have done on a lump of wet clay. Thence, he went back to the Jetavana.

It is in connection with this matter that it is said: "In this very season of Lent (Pu*nn*a) . . . . attained to parinirvā*n*a." [3] (By these words, it must be understood that he reached that state wherein no traces remain of the components of corporeal and

(1) To wit: a relic.

(2) Lit., shewed.

(3) *Vide* text of the *Saññyutta-nikāya* already mentioned.

The two sacred foot-prints always were for the people and the kings in the course of long centuries, a great object of veneration, up to the reign of *Cackôn Ci* Sū Kyo Ta*n* ( စစ်ကိုင်းစည်သူကျော်ထင် ). In his time, fervour and piety seem to have greatly diminished; for, from this reign, the *Shwe-set-taw* (sacred foot-print) was abandoned by degrees, and then completely forgotten, so that in 1590 A.D., no one in Burma seemed to be aware of the existence of the sanctified spot, not even the inhabitants of the Minbu District. This strange neglect is accounted for by the perpetual wars and revolutions of this troubled period. The foot-prints were discovered anew, amid quasi-miraculous circumstances, in the reign of Sālva*n* Ma*n* Tarā, သာလွန်မင်းတရား (1629—1648). On a certain day, the king, hearing the story of Pu*n*na, such as it is in the Pu*nn*ovāda*tth*akathā, which has been given above, ordered informations to be taken about those foot-prints, but nobody could give any. The place was overgrown with thick vegetation, and no one remembered having even heard of them. The king asked the help of the famous bishop To*n* Bhīlā ( တောင်ဘီလာ ). This bishop is the author of the following works: *Vinayālankāratikā sac*, on the *Vinaya*; *Atthasālini ū gāthā aphvan*, a commentary on the first twenty *gāthā* of the *Atthasālini*; *Sālvan Man Tarā amé aphyé*, answers to king Sālvan Ma*n* Tarā's Questions, and *vessantarā pyô*, a metrical version of the *Vessantarajātaka*. He went, accompanied by four other bishops and twelve monks, in search of the famous foot-prints. The king gave them, it is said, a guard of five thousand men to protect them against the Chins (*written* Khya*n*) and the wild Karens (Kara*n* rô*n*, ကရင်ရိုင်း). They left Ava in 1638, carried on red palanquins, went down the Irrawaddy in boats and landed at Minbu. The four bishops camped under a large tree, and in the evening recited prayers and texts from the *Tipitaka*.

mental individuality). The people paid great honours to the remains of the *thera* during seven days and, having gathered a large quantity of fragrant wood, they cremated him, took his relics and erected a shrine (*cetiya*, *Sanskrit* caitya) over them.

To*n* Bhīlā recited long passages from the *Patthāna*, one of the *Abhidhammā* books and retired to sleep very late. At three in the morning, he had a dream. A man holding a spear in his hand and followed by a great black dog, approached him and said: "My Lord, the forests into which you are going to venture are very extensive and very wild; they swarm wtth lions, tigers, panthers and snakes; why do you come here?" The bishop answered: "We are the disciples of Gotama, the Buddha. We learned from the commentary on the Saññyutta-nikāya that the Buddha came to this region and impressed, at the request of a *Nāga* and of a hermit, two marks of his left foot. These imprints, long adored by the Burmese people, have been, owing to wars and revolutions, forgotten and have at last disappeared; at least nobody knows where they are. We have come to look for them." The man said: "My Lord, follow this black dog wherever he goes." And while he was still speaking, To*n* Bhīlā awoke, and told his dream to the other bishops. They took their meal early and entered the forest. And, lo! before them appeared the black dog; he conducted them to the banks of the Ma*n* Kyo*n*, မန်းချောင် (Nammadānadī), and suddenly disappeared. They crossed the torrent and, on the bank they saw a Bhilū (*yakkhu*) seated on the trunk of a tree, who asked them whither they were going; and, on hearing their object, he pointed out to them, with a nod of his head, the hill whereon were the foot-prints. All of a sudden, the guardian-spirit of the hill changed himself into a crow, and, alighting on the very spot where was the sacred relic, attracted, by his peculiar cries and cawings, the attention of the bishops. The foot-print on the summit of the hill was soon discovered, and the bishops, the monks and the soldiers were lost in profound adoration. During the following night, To*n* Bhīlā again recited the Pa*tth*āna, and the spirits of the hills and woods came around him and listened respectfully. "Who are you!" asked the bishop. A Nat (spirit) who was *sotāpanno* (who had entered the First Path) said: "I am a sotāpan (*sotāpanno*) Nat." "Hast thou known the Buddha!" "Yes," said the Nat. "Is my recitation of the Pa*tth*āna," asked the bishop rather vainly, "good? Do I pronounce as the Buddha?" "Ahem! One can, with a deal of good will, guess what thou art reciting," answered the spirit. The pious bishop was incensed; but the Nat soon consoled him and told him to make the resolution to become a Buddha in times to come; so did at once To*n* Bhīlā. He spread his mantle on the foot-print and said: "If it be true that I shall become a Buddha, let the impress of the sacred foot be apparent on my mantle!" It is said that his mantle rose into the air in the form of a heron and, when it came down again, the divine imprint was impressed thereon. The bishop has, since that time, been considered as a *bodhisatta*. They had then to look for the foot-print left on the bank of the stream; that was easy enough, for it sent forth a bright light. A *cetiya* (Burmese ceti, စေတီ), was erected over each foot-print, which, since that time, attracts every year thousands of pilgrims from all parts of Burma.

G. B. C. P. O.—No. 360, Secy., 27-11-06—251—R.W.

www.ingramcontent.com/pod-product-compliance
Lightning Source LLC
Chambersburg PA
CBHW081308040426
42452CB00014B/2705
* 9 7 8 1 5 3 5 8 0 8 0 5 7 *